Good Things Take Time

Ivan King

All situations and events depicted are from the author's perspective and perception. No harm is intended to any person, alive or dead, whom the author knows or has known.

The author reserves all rights. Except for literary reviews, any use of this material, whole or in part, or, referenced in any way by any medium including, but not limited to: electronic, mechanical, or digital copy; and any recording thereof (Auditory, Digital, or Written) is forbidden without prior written permission from the author.

This book, written by Ivan King, is a [Motivational Books] about the many paths the journey of life takes us through.

Good Things Take time

Author: Ivan King
Printed by: Valley Group Media, LLC.
Editing: Jim S. Stein
Cover Art: Tyler D. Masterson
Publisher: Valley Group Media, LLC.
ISBN-13: 978-1515113485
Copyright: Ivan King/ Valley Group Media, LLC.
First Printing: January 25, 2011 United States of America
Copyright © 2015 Ivan King
All rights reserved.

Hear What the Critics are Saying

"Very heart-warming stories; not only was this book inspirational, but it was also incredibly helpful. I would highly recommend it to anyone who is lost and needs to find themselves. **Amazing Book.**"

-Mary Jones -Valley Daily News

"I enjoyed this motivational book quite a bit. My favorite story was the one about the ***Peanut butter And Jelly*** sandwiches. **Five Stars.**"

-Judy B. Cohen –Elite Media Group

"This was a very up-lifting and inspirational book. It both motivated and taught me to think outside of the box. **A Must Read.**"

-Dave Baker -Book Bloggers of America

"I was really moved by some of the stories; what I like about this book is that some of the stories where motivational and others were just about teaching a specific lesson. **Ten Thumbs Up.**"

-Debra Eisner -Literary Times Inc.

"Very inspiring book with great stories; I **Highly Recommend** this one to anybody who likes to read, and whose soul needs a bit of healing."

-Emma Righter -Writers United Group

"I liked a lot of the stories; my favorite was the one about the ***Gumballs***; since I'm in sales, it made a lot of sense to me. This is definitely one book you will not regret buying. **Great Book!**"

-Carl Mosner –Readers Cove Unlimited

Editorial Review

Good Things Take Time is a book that will make you laugh and think at the same time. The way the author explains very complex issues in such a simplistic, *easy-to-comprehend* fashion is commendable.

These are the types of stories that feed our soul. Any generation, young or old, will enjoy this book very much; many of its stories are not only inspiring, but also time tested and true. If you are looking for a book that will not only inspire you, but will also challenge the way you view the world, then this is the book for you. **A Must Read!**

Jim S. Stein

About the Book

If you loved the ***Chicken-Soup for the Soul*** series, then you'll love **Good Things Take Time**. It's a book full of motivational short stories that will not only inspire and motivate you, but will also give you great practical advice on everyday situations.

This book is extremely funny in some parts and yet, very deep and thought provoking in others. It will elicit numerous emotions from its readers and shed more light on solutions to problems we face on a day to day basis. If you're looking for a book that will not only motivate your soul, but will also cultivate your mind, then look no further. **Good Things Take Time** will leave you both inspired and prepared.

Note From the Author

The lessons in this book are told from my perspective. Obviously, certain stories will have distinct meanings to different people; so I will let you be the judge of what each story means to you.

"The Difference between a successful person and others is not a lack of strength, not a lack of knowledge, but rather a lack of will."

Vince Lombardi

Good Things Take Time

Amazon Monkey

There's a small monkey that lives deep within the Amazon jungles of Brazil. They call this monkey the *MACAQUINHO* and it just so happens that these tiny, but dynamic creatures are on the verge of going into extinction. As it were, they're one of the most sought after animals on the black markets that lie between the borders of Brazil and Paraguay.

When the monkeys first began being hunted, the poachers found it very difficult to catch the undersized, but extremely elusive critters; eventually, one poacher came up with a brilliant idea on how to catch the little guys.

It happened one evening when he was observing the captured monkeys eat. He noticed that the *MACAQUINHOS* were exceptionally fond of a particular fruit called *ABACATE*.

This gave the poacher a great idea; so he made a wooden trap and laid several *ABACATE* on the floor of the trap. On one of the sides of the trap he made a small hole. The hole was just big enough for the *MACAQUINHO* to fit his tiny hands through; however, it wasn't large enough for the *ABACATE* to come out. He tied the trap to a tree and then shook it back and forth to make sure that it could resist the pressure of being pulled and tugged on. He then hid behind a bush and waited.

The small monkeys were attracted to the sweet smell of the exotic fruit. Before long, one of these intrepid creatures comes along and begins to observe the wooden trap with wanton curiosity. He sees the sweet scented fruit inside and reaches in for it. To his bewilderment, the sweet fruit wouldn't come out of the cage when he tried to bring it out to eat. He yanked as hard as he could, but the fruit simply wouldn't fit through the tiny hole. As a matter of fact, he pulled so hard he began to bleed from the wrist.

Then, the poacher comes out from hiding, while holding open a netted bag where he is to put the monkey. Alarmed, the monkey sees the man approaching and becomes frantic. Even though all he has to do is let go of the fruit in order to escape, he begins to yank even more profusely so he can get the fruit out. But his efforts are made in vain as the hunter comes along, scoops up the monkey and puts him into the bag.

The poacher does this over and over again; invariably, trapping many *MACAQUINHOS*.

Lesson: Often times we really want to be successful; but unfortunately, we simply are not willing to let go of those bad habits which hold us back, and keeps us from reaching our full potential.

P.B. And J.

John works at a car factory in Detroit. He loves his job; moreover, he loves his friends. He is a model employee and has been working at the same factory ever since he got out of high school. Being one of the guys who has been around the longest, he is well known by his peers.

One wouldn't have to argue with the fact that John's life is fairly routine. Every day he gets up at the same time, goes to work at the same time, and when he is at work, he always does the same repetitive job every day…day in and day out.

It so happened that one day, during lunchtime, he sat at his usual table with some of his coworkers; they talked about football games and sexy secretaries and eventually, one by one, they took out their lunch bags. One guy took out yoghurt, a banana and a sandwich. Another took about a meatballs sub. Ultimately, they all took out somewhat similar homemade lunches.

When it was John's turn, he took out a peanut butter and jelly sandwich. He paused for a brief second when he realized what he had for lunch. A look of complete shock and utter disgust engulfed him. His coworkers noticed this and asked him what was wrong.

"You got someone else's lunch or something?" Asked one friend.

"No, it's just that I hate peanut butter and jelly sandwiches," he replied.

With a very sad puppy eyes look of despair, he began to un-wrap his sandwich. One of his coworkers, feeling a bit sorry for him, handed him half of his Italian cold cut sandwich. Then another followed suit and gave him an apple. Ultimately, they all gave him something of theirs.

"Don't worry we'll share," said one guy.

"That's what friends are for."

The following day, John was the last one to make it to the lunch table. His coworkers greeted him politely as he sat down. Someone was nearing the end of joke and everyone roared with laughter as he delivered the punch line.

Then, one by one, they began to take out their respective lunches; same scenario, different day. No one was really paying attention until someone cried out, "Man I can't believe this!" It was John.

Everyone stared surprisingly at him and almost immediately they noticed the reason for his sudden burst. In his hand, he seemed to be holding yet another peanut butter and jelly sandwich.

"Peanut butter and jelly again!" He cried out in a defeated tone.

Just like the previous day, one by one his friends shared some of their lunch with him so that he wouldn't have to eat the dreaded peanut butter and jelly sandwich.

The next day, during lunch time, no one

greeted John when he sat down at the table. They went about as usual, telling jokes and talking football. Then, time came for everyone to take out their lunches. No one spoke. There was a palpable level of tension in the air. Silently and secretly, everyone was anxious to see what John would take out of his lunch bag.

All of them had their lunch out and waited for John to open his and as he reached into the bag, one colleague, while in mid-bite, actually froze with anticipation.

John just smiled at everyone and slowly took his hand out; but sure enough, he was holding yet another peanut butter and jelly sandwich. He became stricken with grief, almost to the point of crying. But this time around, no one felt pity for him. Now they were annoyed and tired of the same old story; so, one of his upset colleagues turns to him and says: "If you don't like peanut butter and jelly sandwiches, why don't you just ask your wife to prepare you something different?"

"But I'm not married," replies John.

"Well, then tell your mother not to prepare them!" Exclaims another.

"I don't live with my mother," he responded to the other.

"Then who the hell prepares your lunches?" Asks a third.

He replies, "I do."

Lesson: You may not be too happy with the life you have, but just remember: You are the owner of the choices you make; you are the architect of your own life. So if you don't like what you see, then change and do something with your life that's worth the while.

Boy Wonder

A child psychologist was doing a study on the early effects of child development when it came to parental influences. Having personally interviewed more than one hundred children, he was almost done with his research and now, was down to the last three.

He buzzed for his secretary and asked her to bring in the first of the three children. A few minutes later the secretary came back holding a little girl's hand, the psychologist grabbed his clipboard, a pen and walked over to the little girl. He took out a lollipop from his pocket and told her not to worry because he was only going to ask her a few questions. He asked her if that would be ok and she nodded that it was. He asked her the series of question and took notes on his clipboard with each answer that she gave him.

Wrapping up his set of questions he asked the little girl, "What do you want to be when you grow up?" She responded right away," I want to be a ballerina when I grow up." As a final question the psychologist asked her why she wanted to be a ballerina and to that, she responded, "Because ballerinas are beautiful and when I grow up I want to be beautiful." On the sheet next to her name, there was a column and in that column the psychologist wrote in the word: *AVERAGE*. Then, he buzzed the secretary once again and asked her to bring in the next child.

This time the secretary brought in a little boy. The doctor sat him down and explained the same thing to him and also gave him a lollipop. He asked the little boy all of the same questions and when he asked him what he wanted to be when he grew up, the little boy, with his chest held high responded, "I want to be a doctor." When he asked the little boy why he wanted to be a doctor he replied, "Because doctors make lots of money and when I grow up I want to be rich." Next to that boys name he also wrote in the word *AVERAGE*.

When the last child came in, the doctor immediately noticed that this case was going to be different from that of the other children because this little boy was blind. So he went on to explain the same things to the little blind boy and also gave him a lollipop before going forward with the interview.

When he asked the little blind boy what he wanted to be when he grew up, the little boy thought about it for a second and then said, "I don't know yet, but I know I am going to be successful in whatever it is that I decide to do."

The psychologist was taken aback by the little boy's level of maturity and confidence so he asked him how he could be so sure that he was going to be successful.

To that, the little boy responded, "That's simple; I know that I am going to be successful because I am blind."

The little boy's answer really took the psychologist by surprise and he failed to comprehend why the little boy thought that being blind could somehow help him to be more successful in life, so with a look of utter bewilderment etched upon his face, he stared at the little boy and asked, "Why do you think that?"

The little boy veered in the direction of the doctor's voice and responded, "Because unlike everyone else, I am incapable of seeing my obstacles."

The doctor was stunned and next to that boy's name he wrote in the word: *GENIUS*.

Lesson: If you don't put too much focus on the negatives surrounding you, then you will most certainly have a better chance of reaching your goals; consequently, if you only happen to see obstacles in your path, then sooner or later you will completely lose the ability to see your objective.

Fruit Vender

A certain man had worked his entire adult life as a janitor at a local high school. Then, unexpectedly, he found himself unemployed because the school was closing due to insufficient government funding. So the man bought a newspaper in order to start the arduous process of job hunting. A couple of days later, he reads a story in the newspaper on how Microsoft was expanding its corporate headquarters; consequently opening some satellite offices in his town.

This news couldn't have come at a better time the man thought. He was certain that they would need someone to be the janitor of the new building; so he decided that he would go in for a job interview. The man went and got himself a professional haircut; he put on his best suit and tie and even got his dress shoes shined and finally, went off to the interview. He was desperate to get another job because he had to pay bills and support his family.

When he gets to the interview, the Microsoft manager asks him some basic questions about past experiences and references, then towards the end, the manager asks him for his email address so he could send him a letter by e-mail informing him if he was going to be hired or not.

The man apologetically explained that he didn't have an e-mail address because he didn't know how to use a computer. "The only thing that I know is how to be a janitor and anything having to do with that job," he explained to the manager.

The Microsoft manager was shocked. "How could someone not have an e-mail address," he thought. Then he proceeded to tell the man that he couldn't be hired by the company because this was Microsoft and they simply couldn't hire anyone who didn't have an email address or didn't know anything about computers.

Understandably, the man was very

disappointed when he walked out of the interview. On his way home, he was wondering how in the world he was going to be able to provide for his family. He had a very little amount of money left and he had to stretch that money out as far as he possibly could, until he found another job.

He went to a nearby Farmers' Market and bought a sack full of oranges with part of the money that he had in savings. The whole sack only cost twenty dollars and it had one hundred oranges in it and with that, he could feed his family for the rest of the week. So he grabbed the sack and began his long journey home.

As he was walking home with the sack of oranges strapped to his back, a woman was coming out of her house and when she saw him, she yelled out, "Hey orange man, orange man!"

When the man turned around, she asked him how much he was selling the oranges. "I'm not really selling these oranges," he began to explain to her. She looked at him somewhat skeptically and then offered him a dollar for each one.

The man just couldn't say no to that, so he

flung the sack full of oranges around and asked her how many she wanted; the woman asked him for twenty. He handed her the oranges and she gave him a twenty dollar bill. The man couldn't believe his luck because he had just made back his own money. A couple of seconds later, a man driving by saw that he had sold oranges to the lady so he stopped his car by the man and asked to buy some oranges as well.

This gave the ex-janitor a great idea, so he went around the neighborhood selling his fresh Tropicana oranges door to door. By the end of the day, he had one hundred dollars in his pocket; making a nice eighty dollar profit margin.

So he did this everyday for a couple of years. Eventually, with the money he saved, he was selling the oranges out of pickup trucks that went around to many different neighborhoods; a siren would let people know that their fresh oranges had arrived.

Not long after that, the ex-janitor, now turned fruit entrepreneur, had his own stand in the Farmers' Market; then, not long after that, he was opening his own fruit stands all over the county. After twenty years he was the most important fruit entrepreneur in the entire state.

One day, an accountant came to give the man an estimate on a job. When he was done, in a business like fashion he looked at the man and said: "I will send you my estimate by e-mail."

The man looked at the accountant and responded, "I don't have an email account."

The accountant was shocked. "How is it possible that the most successful fruit entrepreneur in the state does not have an email account?" He asked in amazement.

The man looked at the accountant and said, "If I had an e-mail account, I would be working as a janitor right now."

Lesson: Never focus on what you don't have; because sometimes, by not having things, is how you end up getting things.

Three Brothers

Three brothers work together in a local merchandising company. One Monday, the mother of the three goes down to the company's main offices in order to speak to her sons' manager. When she got to the waiting room, a secretary, told her to take a seat and that the manager would be with her as soon as he got off a phone call.

A couple of minutes later, a tall and very sharp looking man wearing a business suit came out of the office. The mother looked over at him as he walked towards her and introduced himself.

"Please come into my office," he motioned for her to go first.

"Darlene, bring us two coffees please." He

said, looking over to his secretary.

As they walked into the office the manager motioned for the mother to take a seat in the nice cushioned leather chair in front of his desk. The woman sat down, but she seemed to be somewhat displeased.

The manager told her that it was a pleasure to finally meet her and then he asked her what he could help her with.

I am concerned about my boys," she begins to explain.

"What about them?" Asked the manager?

"Well, it's just that all three of them got hired here the same day, all of them have been here the same amount of time, work the same amount of hours and even have the same positions….

"Ok and that's a problem for you?" Asked the manager.

"No, it's not that." She continued to explain, "What I don't understand is, if they all have the same positions and do the same amount of work why do they all make different amounts of money?"

The manager listened to her quietly and fully understood her concerns.

He began to explain it to her, but then decided that it would be easier to show her why there was a significant difference in the three salaries.

On the intercom he calls down to the warehouse and asks to speak to the first son. When he answers, the manager asks him about the shipment that was supposed to have arrived that morning. The first son mumbled something to the extent of not knowing anything about any shipment.

Then the manager called down and asked for the second son and when he came on, the manager also asked him about the shipment. This son at least knew of the shipment, however, he couldn't confirm whether it had arrived or not. But he was going to find out and later inform the manager.

Then the manager called down for the third and final son. When the manager asked him about the shipment he seemed to know all about it.

"Yes sir, it arrived this morning. I did inventory on it and found that it's a crate short but, don't worry sir, I already sent a fax to the company's corporate office and they are replacing the crate within the next shipment. Furthermore, I sent some of the new merchandize out to do a test market and found an adequate price point. Selling it at this price point, minus the cost of the product, including shipping and taxes will leave us with better than expected profits. Also, I did a sales analysis and at the going rate we will run out of merchandize within two weeks, but I have already sent out a new order form. Don't worry about what's going on down here sir," continued the last son, "I got everything under control."

The manager turns to the mother and says, "Now do you see why they make different amounts of money?"

Lesson: Having mentality is what makes a person successful, not their position. And sometimes, what separates your salary from somebody else's, is the thoroughness and attitude with which you decide to do your job.

The Office

Dex is the most successful person amongst his friends and family members. He has everything that anyone could ever want; the luxury cars, the beautiful houses, heck, he even has his own helicopter. Everybody desires to be like Dex. Undeniably, men aspire to be like him and women want to be with him.

Dex has an assistant that follows him everywhere like a personal slave. One day, his assistant admiringly looks at him and says, "Sir, no matter what it takes, I want to be exactly like you. I'm willing to do everything that you had to do, if it means getting to where you are today!"

He stares at his assistant in amusement and replies, "Do you know why everyone calls me Dex?"

The assistant shot him an instant look of confusion. He had never really given much thought into the origins of his boss's name, but always assumed that it was the name given to him at birth. Seeing his assistant's confused reaction to the question, he offers the information.

"My real name is Dan Epstein, and as you are well aware, I began working in this company when I got out of college." He paused for a couple of seconds while he dug up old thoughts from his past.

He continued, "When I first began working here, I was the worst employee this company had ever seen," he looked over to his assistant to see how he was reacting to all the news.

The assistant had a look of complete disbelieve etched upon his face.

"As I was saying," he continued with his story. "I was the worst employee because I was full of excuses; what I'm trying to get at is that I had an excuse for everything."

"I never got any of my projects done in time but expectantly, I always came up with a different excuse for why that was. My teams never met their goals, but not to worry, because I had an excuse for that as well. Then, one morning the head of my department had a meeting with all of the staff because he was very displeased with the overall performance of the office. He let everyone have it, especially me.......

The assistant was now listening with a lot more interest. He just couldn't wrap his mind around the thought of his boss being anything else but the best example, much less irresponsible.

…..and he really let me have it too. In front of everyone he yelled at me. He went on and on about how I was full of excuses and that he couldn't count on me for anything. He said I had so many excuses that I was like a rolodex of excuses; that in fact, he was going to nickname me Rolodex."

Dex looked over to his assistant who seemed utterly shocked at the story he had just heard.

"So Dex," he continued, "is really short for Rolodex."

"If that's true, than how did you get to be where you are today? I mean, now you run the entire company!" Exclaimed the assistant.

"Well, from that day on, every time someone made fun of my excuse giving abilities, I got angry, so eventually, I stopped using excuses and simply started getting things done. The rest is history. The nick name stuck, but I like it because it reminds me of where I came from and most importantly, how I got to be where I am today."

Lesson: Everyone has a theory on why they aren't where they should be; news flash, those aren't theories they're excuses and the sooner you stop using them, the quicker you will get to be where you want to be.

Wiseman and King

A powerful King was disturbed by the rumors that there was a wise man somewhere in his Kingdom that had the ability to tell the future and also, the power to read men's minds. The King felt that this wise man posed a threat to his sovereignty, so he wanted to devise a way to kill the wise man without converting him into a martyr; ultimately, to discredit him as well as kill him. One day, he came up with a brilliant plan.

The King ordered the guards to go out and find this wise man, so that he could be brought before the King's "Court" in order to be tested.

A couple of days later, the guards arrive with a very timid and tired looking old man.

The King couldn't believe that this was the man that so many had spoken about. He ordered the old man forward and the man fearfully took several steps towards the King.

The king escorted him to a table in one corner of the room. On the table lay four closed jars. Taking a step towards the wise man, the King began to tell him all the things that he had heard about self proclaimed seer. That supposedly he was very wise because he was able to see into the future and also that he could read men's minds.

The man looked up in silence neither confirming nor denying what the King had heard about him.

Giving him a stern look, the King pointed to the jars and explained to the wise man that three out of the four jars contained certain death.

One jar was filled with the deadliest spiders of the Amazon and that a single bite from even the smallest spider would shut down ones nervous system within seconds and that death, would follow almost immediately after that.

The second jar, he went on to explain, was filled with the most poisonous scorpions of the Sahara desert. Even the softest prick would be enough to kill a man in mere seconds.

Accordingly, the third jar was filled with the most venomous snakes of Indonesia. A single bite would shoot venom straight to the heart and all the vital organs would become useless in less than an hour. The wise man swallowed hard and took a deep breath as he heard all of this.

Ultimately, the King explained to him what was in the fourth jar; it was filled with gold coins and precious rubies.

Then, smiling at his own cleverness, the King shot the wise man a cold stare and told him that he would have to make a choice, by reaching into one of the jars. If he chose the right jar, then he would be richer than he had ever imagined; but if he chose the wrong jar, then he would choose certain death.

The wise man looked back towards the door

to see if he had yet another option and he noticed that the guards had their swords pointing towards him.

He turned to face the jars and took another big nervous swallow. He walked around the table several times fretfully looking down on the jars.

As he waited with anticipation, the mighty King sat on his thrown, feeling very proud of his astuteness.

After several long, pressure filled minutes the wise man stopped in front of one of the jars, opened the lid and without any hesitation, reached in with his eyes closed.

To his disbelief, he moved his hand around, as he fondled all the gold coins and precious rubies. Abruptly, the wise man turned to the king and said, "A wise man isn't one that can see into the future, or one that can read men's minds; a wise man is one that reaches out for opportunity, even at the risk of losing his life."

He grabbed his jar of riches and walked out of the room leaving the King, sitting speechless, on his thrown.

Lesson: Opportunities don't come around very often, so make sure that you grab hold of it when it does and when you do have a hold of it, be certain that you do whatever it takes in order to maximize its full potential.

Glass Factory

Joe had spent a significant part of his life working in a glass factory. His life was pretty systematic; he had the same routine every day, same work schedule, same friends and even the same old stories.

Consistently, Joe's friends would have to listen to him complain and ramble on and on about how someday he was going to do something big with his life.

One day, over lunch, Joe announces to his coworkers that at any moment he was going to quit, because he was going to open up his own business. He went on to explain that he was only waiting for his mother-in-law to move out of his house and then, he and his wife were going to take whatever money they had in savings and open up their own business.

Then, the day came when Joe's mother in law moved out. But now he had a baby on the way, so he told his friends that he was going to have to stay put until the baby was born; but as soon as that happened, he was going to quit…he assured them. "I'm going to open my own business." He echoed emphatically.

Quite a few years later, that same baby was getting ready to attend high school so Joe, who still rambled consistently about opening up his own business, told his colleagues that it wasn't possible yet, because he had to wait until his daughter was out of the house and into college.

Years later, Joe's little girl got an acceptance letter into a fine institution so Joe definitely could not set out on an entrepreneurial adventure because now he was going to have to help his daughter with college tuition. But nevertheless, he defiantly talked about opening up his own business.

Finally, the day came when Joe's little girl was graduating from college and she surprised the entire family by announcing that she was engaged to be married.

So once again Joe had to push his own

plans aside because he had to help out with the wedding. But he swore that as soon as the honeymoon was over he was going to immediately quit his job in order to open up his own business.

But the real shock came when his daughter announced that she was pregnant. So once more, Joe had to put his plans on the shelf.

"Ohh, but as soon as my grandson is born I am out of here," he assured his colleagues.

Anyway, to make a long story short, this kept going on and on, year after year. Until a day came in which Joe could no longer open up his own business because he was six feet under.

Lesson: We have all heard the cliché: don't put things off to till the last minute. Think about it, do you really want to be that old guy or gal that always complains about how they wish they would have done this or that? In truth, it would only take us half the time to actually do the things that we consistently waste so much time talking about doing.

MR. Tamaguchi

Mr. Tamaguchi is one of the world's most powerful and successful Japanese businessmen. As it would have it, he was making a trip to America to check on some of his business investments. He was staying at a five star hotel with a beach side view. The private suite where he was staying just happened to cost fifteen thousand dollars a night.

The suite was something truly spectacular, but the best thing about it was its view. He was right on the beach where he could see the ocean's beautiful, clear blue waters for miles and miles.

One morning, dozens of reporters had gathered in order to interview Mr. Tamaguchi for their respective magazines or newspapers. The interview was conducted in a private office that had been set up specifically for Mr.

Tamaguchi. As only he would have it, more than ten separate phone lines had installed so that he could receive important phone calls from all of his different business associates from around the world.

The reporters were extremely excited about interviewing a man that was as powerful and successful as Mr. Tamaguchi; they were bursting with anticipation to ask him all kinds of questions.

When Mr. Tamaguchi arrived, he immediately opened the floor up for questioning and one of the first reporters to raise his hands was called upon.

The reporter stood up and asked, "Mr. Tamaguchi, is it true that you know everything there is to know about being successful and ultimately, being happy?"

He responded by saying that he was the most successful Japanese businessman in the world and that yes he knew everything there was to know about the secrets to the lifelong pursuit of happiness.

The reporter quickly asked him a follow up

question, "Mr. Tamaguchi, can you tell me what you see outside?"

This question caught Mr. Tamaguchi by surprise because he was expecting questions concerning business and questions about his personal life; nevertheless, he turned around and looked out into the open waters of the ocean.

He spent several long minutes looking up and down the beach and at the ocean and everywhere else; then he turned to the reporter and said, "That's easy, there's nothing outside."

The reporter, somewhat perplexed, says to Mr. Tamaguchi, "Sir are you absolutely sure that there is nothing outside, please check again?"

Mr. Tamaguchi turned around and looked again; he looked down at the beach and saw no shops, no restaurants, no malls, not even any cars. He looked out at the ocean and saw no boats or cruise liners and looked up at the sky and saw no planes or helicopters so he turned back to the reporter and once again said that he saw nothing.

The reporter was amazed at the way Mr. Tamaguchi viewed the world around him and so he asked, "Sir, do you not see the ocean, look at all the shades of green and blue in the water. Do you not see how beautiful it is? What about the young lovers holding hands on the beach do you not see them? How about the flocks of birds flying in the distance are they invisible to you as well? And those fluffy, magnificently shaped clouds and look at how beautiful the day is! Sir, do you not see all this beauty in nature?"

Mr. Tamaguchi was shocked by all of this and he was surprised to learn of the horrible way in which he looked at the world. He was only able to recognize things that had a physical value. The realization of this saddened him deeply, so he cancelled all the meetings he had scheduled and spent the remainder of his day strolling on the beach, taking his time to admire all of the beauty that surrounded him.

Lesson: Don't let your personal development become limited to only economical growth, because we can also grow morally and spiritually; remember, there are a myriad of things in life that are valuable, so don't get caught up on judging yourself or the those around you only by what they own physically.

Thief of the Stars

A thief became incredibly famous because the cops could not do anything to stop or catch this guy. He first began by robbing regular people's homes, but when that stopped being challenging he started robbing the homes of the rich and famous.

Almost once a week he would hit a different house. The media dubbed him, "Burglar of the Stars." Everywhere you looked, on talk shows and in the news, the thief was being talked about. Famous comedians made jokes about him and politicians and law men vowed to catch him.

The robber got to be so famous that some people actually wished they would become one of his victims, because he only robbed the rich and famous, which meant that you definitely had to be someone important to be robbed by this guy. I mean if you were just a regular Joe there was no way that the "Burglar of the Stars" would come into your home.

One day, something miraculous happened, they actually caught the bandit. It happened on a Saturday night, he broke into a famous football player's house thinking that he was away on a game, but what he didn't know was that the football star had hired a security company to protect his house. The thief triggered a silent alarm and in a matter of minutes was surrounded by more than fifty cops.

On Monday, a news conference was held and the mayor made the announcement that everyone was waiting for, "The 'Burglar of the Stars' has been finally apprehended and is now behind bars awaiting trial."

When the cops searched his home, they found almost everything that he had stolen during his spree of crimes. They even found a set of paintings that were valued at more than one million dollars, but the cops didn't have any report about stolen paintings so they confronted the thief about it.

The burglar explained to the cops that he was not always a thief; before he was a painter, but he never had success in that field and that was how he began his life of crime. When he found out how much money his paintings were worth he couldn't believe it.

After his trial and subsequent sentence he was interviewed by a famous reporter from one of these big name-network stations and one of the questions that the reporter asked him was, "Who was the biggest person that you have ever robbed?

The, could have been a great painter, but instead was now the ex thief of the rich and famous, turned to the cameras and said, "Myself."

Lesson: Don't ever give up on yourself and your dreams. You just never know, reaching the ultimate goal might just be around the corner and, no matter what; you should never lose faith in that.

Personal Genie

One fortuitous morning, a young man was walking along a dirt road kicking up gravel as he went along. Suddenly, when he kicked a small patch of dirt, he saw the sharp end of something sticking out from the ground. He dug it up to reveal a lamp of some kind.

At first glance, he thought that it was a run-of-the-mill oil lamp. But upon closer inspection, he noticed that the lamp had strange markings on its side. It looked to be written in some archaic language so he couldn't understand what it said.

Then, he remembered the well known story

of the Genie in the Bottle. Even though he didn't believe in such tall tales, he still thought that it would be pretty funny to rub it to see if a Genie would come out. So he rubbed the side of the lamp ferociously.

Unsuspectingly, a puff of smoke shot straight up into the air and an intimidating huge man hovered high above him. The giant man began to stretch his arms as though he had just woken from a thousand year long sleep.

The young man simply couldn't believe what he was seeing. "As I live and breathe; a real life Genie!" He thought out loud. At first he was just in shock and didn't really know what to think. Eventually, he remembered all the stories told of the genie; mainly how, when freed, they would have to grant you three wishes. The young man's mind began to race with anticipation and excitement. He waited until the Genie focused before asking him for his three wishes. After a long, much needed stretch, the Genie looked down to see who had freed him. That's when he saw the young man smiling and staring up at him.

"You have freed me and for that, I will

grant you three wishes," proclaimed the genie.

"Absolutely anything that I want?" Asked the young man, feeling somewhat skeptic.

"Anything," responded the Genie.

The young man looked deep within himself and began to think of all the things he has ever wanted. A tsunami of ideas flooded his mind.

Then he looked up at the giant figure and said: "I want to be filthy rich, I want to be successful, and above all, I want to be someone that is considered powerful in the business world."

The young man stood back and waited for the Genie's response.

The Genie looked down upon the man and told him, "I will make all of your wishes come true, but there are four things that I will ask of you before I grant you these wishes. If you do these four things for a period of ten years, then I will come back and grant all your wishes."

The young man immersed himself into deep thought. Maybe he was not going to like these four things that he had to do or, what if they were four things that he could not do and he was going to have to do them for ten years. He was leaning towards telling the Genie no, but his curiosity and ambition got the best of him so he asked, "What are these four things that I have to do?"

"Well, I want you to set up your own business, it doesn't matter what kind of business, but whatever it is that you do, you have to apply these four rules that I am going to give you and if you do them for a period of ten years then I will grant your wishes."

"Ok, that sounds simple enough," responds the young man.

"The first of these things is *DESIRE:* you have to desire success so much that you will be willing to do whatever it takes in order to obtain it. The second is *DETERMINATION:* you have to be determined to succeed because you will face many obstacles along the way. The third is *DEDICATION:* you have to be committed to your business, so every day you are to be the first one to arrive and you will be the last one to leave. The last thing is *DISCIPLINE:* you will discipline yourself with nothing but the best of habits and you will have to become the hardest working person you know.

The young man once again immersed himself into deep thought; then, he looked up decidedly and shook hands with the Genie in agreement. Without warning, the Genie disappeared loudly echoing, "See you in ten years."

So the young man went to work on setting up his own business. He didn't have any money to invest, so he simply took out an old lawn mower from his shed and walked around the neighborhood offering lawn cutting services to all his neighbors.

Every day the young man was up at the crack of dawn and everyday he worked his finger to the bone till it was completely dark outside. Before long, he was cutting every single person's lawn in the neighborhood. He saved enough money to buy himself a truck, also new and better lawn care equipment. As time passed, his business expanded, he had more than twenty landscaping trucks and he had thousands of clients all throughout the state. Ultimately, he became the most powerful landscape contractor in the state.

In his seventh year in business he made his first million. By the tenth year he was already a multi, multi millionaire. One afternoon, he was sitting in his big office downtown, when out of nowhere the Genie reappeared before his eyes.

The man was taken back in surprise. His level of commitment to the company was so consuming that he had forgotten all about the Genie. Then he remembered the deal they had made with one another ten years earlier. The man knew that he had done everything that the Genie had asked of him; all the same, he was a little disappointed to see him.

Noticing the sad look upon the man's face, the Genie asked to the-now successful businessman, "What's wrong? I thought you would be happy to see me, because I come to grant you your wishes."

"Yes, and I thank you for keeping your word, but the truth is, I don't need your help anymore because I already have everything I ever wanted. I am so rich that I don't even know how I am going to spend all my money. I am the most successful person I know and my company is the most powerful landscaping company in the state. So maybe you can pass on those wishes on to someone who really needs them," explained the man.

The Genie was not surprised by all this and then, just as quickly as he had appeared, he disappeared once again.

Lesson: You are your own personal genie; all you have to do is apply the four D's of success to your personal and professional life and you will be endowed with the power to make all your wishes come true.

Gumball Theory

A teacher and his student were at the airport waiting for a plane when the student turned to the teacher and asked him what it was that he needed to do to succeed in life.

The teacher thought about the question for a while and quickly looked around the airport waiting room to see what he could find. When he spotted what it was that he was looking for, he got up and asked his student to follow him. Together they walked over to a gumball machine.

Standing in front of it, the teacher asked the student to estimate how many gumballs were in the machine. The student examined the machine carefully and responded by saying, "About a hundred give or take a few."

"Ok," says the teacher. "Let's say that there are one hundred gumballs in this machine. Let's also say that all of them are of different colors and there are many of each color. But, hypothetically, there is only one blue gumball in this entire machine. Now it costs one quarter for you to take out one gumball does it not?"

The student looked down on the machine to make sure and responded. "It does."

"Well, let's say that I give you one hundred quarters and tell you that I want you to deposit each quarter in the machine, but with only one single objective and that is to get the blue gumball. Now, do you think that it's possible to get to the blue gumball with the first quarter?"

"Yeah it's possible, but very unlikely," responded the student.

"Exactly, but if you spend the day putting every single quarter into the machine, then it's safe to say that at the end of the day you will have your blue gumball, you will also have ninety nine other gumballs of different colors, but all the same, you will have the blue gumball as well."

"That's just like success. If it doesn't happen on the first try, then you just have to keep on trying until you get it right and you just may have to go through ninety nine failures before you get to your first success.

Lesson: You should never give up on your dreams. If you want to be successful in whatever you choose to do, then you have to have resolve and most of all, *stickativity* to persevere through the tough times.

Tree of Knowledge

In the city of Okinawa, Japan, there was a sacred tree affectionately named the Tree of Corin. The tree was very sacred to the town's people because the tree was older than the town itself.

The Tree of Corin stood ten meters high and had a trunk that was about two meters in diameter; the tree was enormous.

All things considered, the town's people pampered the tree as though it were a person and not just any person, but rather the most import person in town. Timed with adequate water cycles, they set up sprinklers around the tree. They also had the best fertilizers brought in from overseas in order to keep the tree healthy. All in all, everything and anything was done to assure the well being of this tree.

One day, the town's people began to notice that the tree was looking different and it wasn't a good type of different. So they began to work overtime in different shifts to take better care of the tree. However, the tree kept getting worse as more and more of its leaves fell to the ground every day. The branches began to dry up and become bridle, eventually breaking apart from the tree and falling to the ground.

The tree, becoming sickened, broke the hearts of the town's people as they felt powerless in their attempt to nurture it back to health. They tried everything, but nothing seemed to work.

So the town's mayor sent for a group of scientist from different fields to come and analyze the tree to see what was wrong with it. But that didn't seem to make much of a difference and no one seemed to be able to figure out why the tree was dying.

One day, a curious team of scientists from England came to study the tree. They brought with them the most advanced, modern equipment available. One such equipment was an extremely powerful microscope, a prototype, the only one of its kind.

The English scientists cut off a small piece

of the tree, set it under the microscope and began to examine the bark with its extremely powerful lens. At first, they were unable to see anything out of the ordinary, but when the microscope was zoomed to its full capacity, they immediately found the culprit behind the tree's demise.

The tiniest little insect, undetectable by the human eye, was what was causing that giant tree to die slowly.

Eventually, the scientists were able to mix the right type of chemicals in order to kill the small critters and therefore, the tree was spared.

Lesson: Occasionally, even the most insignificant of things can bring a giant to its knees. So make sure that you always pay extra attention to every detail, because even the smallest thing that isn't done right can keep you or your company from reaching goals.

Yard Sale Guy

John was an accountant for a local accounting firm. His job was unbearably boring; adding insult to injury, he made minimal wage, so understandably, he hated his job. It was a regular nine to five type gig and he made roughly twelve hundred dollars a month.

On weekends, John spent most of his time going to yard sales with his older sister. He liked going to yard sales with her because she was so passionate about them. She even had a whole technique down for finding yard sales; her system was simple enough, she would buy several newspapers and cut out the different ads for yard sales, then she would map them out and mark the quickest paths to get to each individual yard sale. He found the whole process to be very relaxing and, truth be told, somewhat exciting.

One day, he was at a yard sale with his sister when he was struck with a great idea.

So when Monday came around, John quit his job. Obviously his family became deeply concerned. It was completely out of character for him to do something so out of the ordinary and they worried that he was having some sort of mental break down. To make matters worse, his family had lots of debt and bills to pay; so being out of a job was only going to make life that much more difficult.

After that, John did something even nuttier, he took the fifteen hundred dollars from their family savings account and then, he began going from yard sale to yard sale buying anything that he could find for fifty cents or less.

John did this for a period of about three weeks and amassed himself over three thousand different items of other people's "junk".

His family became increasingly concerned. Then, in the beginning of the forth week John began to put up flyers all over his neighborhood announcing that there was going to be a giant yard sale over the weekend. He put signs everywhere; at schools, supermarkets, bus stops and, not leaving anything to chance, he also put ads in the local newspaper.

On the day of the yard sale, all throughout the yard, John set out signs that read: "Anything and everything for a dollar."

Then he set up a table, pulled up a chair, put a money box on top of the table and waited for the customers to arrive.

By the end of the weekend John had sold more than three thousand different items that he himself had bought in other yard sales. This gave him a gross profit of three thousand dollars and a net profit of fifteen hundred, a total of three hundred dollars more than he would have made at his old job.

John did this for several months, eventually offering more and more items for sale. Before long, he was doing his yard sales every other Saturday and Sunday of the month.

He began to have lots of success with his sales; maybe just a bit too much, because the neighbors began to complain about all the noise, commotion and traffic that was caused by the enormous amount of people coming from everywhere.

So John, with the money he had saved over the years, opened up his own thrift shop and before long he opened another, then another, and within years of first starting out, he owned more than a dozen shops all over the state. Eventually, he became a millionaire in the thrift business.

The name of his shops: *THE JUNK YARD*

Lesson: Most of the times in life, opportunities simply don't come up and slap you in the face; so be innovative and create your own dynamic brand of success.

Flying Xanadu

One sunny afternoon a certain monk was out in the fields getting ready to start his chores. On this particular day he was instructed to clear a piece of land so that the next day the other monks, who were in charge of planting, could lay seeds down.

The monk walked lazily to the middle of the field and threw his hoe hastily onto the ground. As he looked up half squinting into the blaring sun, he wiped the sweat from his face with his left hand and shuddered his eyes with his right.

"It was way too hot to be working out in the

fields," thought the monk depressingly. Then, he quickly surveyed the vast piece of land that he was going to have to clear and plow. He sighed at the mere thought of all that work. Frustrated, he kicked a rough patch of dirt that was directly in front of him.

"This dirt is way too hard to plow, this is going to take me forever," continuing his diatribe, "There's absolutely no way that I'm going to get this done by the end of the day!" He complained bitterly.

In that precise moment, a gigantic dragon named Xanadu came flying down from the heavens. With a thunderous roar he landed right in front of the bickering monk. The dragon fixed its own eyes upon the monk and smoke began to come out of his nostrils.

The monk fell to his knees with fear. He was shaking all over and wanted to run away but was too scared stiff to do so.

Xanadu looked down on the quivering monk and ordered him to stand up. The monk was fearful for his life, but did exactly as he was told.

"I want you to bring me some things and if you do exactly as I command you, I will spare your life," said the towering dragon.

The monk, still shaking responded, "Anything that you ask for I shall do, Sir great dragon but please don't eat me!"

"You fool! You think that I would risk indigestion by eating a despicable worm like you," bellowed the dragon; and as he finished his sentence, more smoke came out of his nostrils, completely blinding the monk.

Stricken with fright, the monk fell to his knees once again and began to beg for forgiveness and mercy.

Xanadu was now growing impatiently at the monk and he told him once again what he wanted, "I want you to bring me an egg, a pouch or bag of any kind, and a hammer." He continued, "If you bring these things to me quickly, then I will spare your life."

The monk rose up hurriedly and darted off to get the things the dragon had asked of him. A few minutes later, he reappears with everything the dragon wanted and, bowing respectfully, he set it in front of one of his giant paws.

The dragon ordered the monk to put the egg into the bag and the monk did so.

Then he ordered the monk to smash the bag with the hammer several times and the monk did so until the egg was completely crushed.

The monk looked up, humbly awaiting the dragon's next command.

The dragon looked down, towards the monks face and asked, "What have you learned from this exercise?"

The monk drew a blank as he looked up at the dragon with a look of utter confusion.

"You fool!" Xanadu yelled down to the monk, "The egg represents your life, the bag represents the pessimism that engulfs your world; throwing it into complete darkness and despair, and the hammer represents the inevitable fate that will befall you if you insist on this path of self destruction." With that being said, the dragon suddenly swooped high up into the clouds and disappeared from sight.

The monk was awed by what had happened

and from that day on, he never uttered or thought anything negative ever again; needless to say, he lived to a very fruitful old age.

Lesson: Life is entirely too short for you to be wasting time on negativity and pessimism. Here is a good rule of thumb to follow: if you don't having anything positive to say then don't say anything and above all, keep your head up and be optimistic about your situation, because you never know when it's going to change for the better.

Golden Rules

Two businessmen ran different advertising firms in the same city. However, one company was tremendously more successful than the other. The guy who ran the successful company was Jim and the other guy was Bob.

Bob couldn't understand why Jim's company was more successful than his. It truly befuddled him because they were both in the same city, sold the same type of service and even had similar pricing.

There were even a lot of similarities between the two managers. They had both attended the same college, they were both married and they were exactly the same age; so Bob spent many a nights pondering why his counterpart was more successful than him.

But no matter how hard he tried, he could never figure it out, so one day he hired a corporate spy to penetrate Jim's company in order find out for him.

The corporate spy went and worked an entire year under Jim taking pages after pages of notes.

Then, one day the spy quit Jim's company and went back to share with Bob all of the information he had gathered on the differences between the two companies.

The spy started out by telling Bob that there were no big differences; no smoking gun that pointed out why one company was so much more powerful and successful than the other.

The spy, however, did note one thing that was unusual. Bob looked anxiously at his spy as though he held the secret to life itself. Then the spy handed Bob a piece of paper with a heading on top, it read: The three golden rules; then beneath that there were three indentations the first of these read: *out work everyone*, the next read: *always have a winning attitude* and the final indentation read: *don't be afraid to ask questions.*

Before he even looked up, the spy went on to say that Jim applied these three golden rules to every facet of his company. He made sure that everyone knew and followed these simple rules; from top executives, down to the guy in the mail room and even to the rookie employee that was on his very first day. Furthermore, all of the employee evaluations were derived from their understanding and execution of the three golden rules he added.

Bob looked up in disbelief. He refused to accept that this was the big secret to Jim's success. He crumpled the piece of paper and threw it into the trash can. A few years after that, Jim bought Bob's company and the first thing that he did as the new boss was: fire the old one.

Lesson: Just like building, every business and business person needs a foundation. At the end of the day that's what's going to make you or your company a strong player in such a global and fluctuating market place.

The Rooster

One Sunday afternoon, a rooster was walking along the forest with his friend the dog, when out of nowhere the sky got extremely dark and all signs pointed to a coming storm. So they quickly began looking for a place where they could spend the night protected from the rain.

About a hundred yards away, the rooster spotted a large tree and on the bottom part of its trunk there was a large hole. So they walked over and climbed into the hole. The inside of the trunk was hollow so the rooster flew up to the top of the tree and rested on a branch hidden by its thick foliage.

In the morning, a hungry fox was sniffing around the woods desperately looking for something…anything to eat. He hadn't eaten in days and was truly starving.

At the crack of dawn, the rooster began to do what all roosters do when the sun comes up and so as loud as he possibly could, the rooster began to crow.

The fox was suddenly startled by the intruding sound; he looked around and saw nothing. Then he walked towards the protruding sound and a couple of minutes later he was looking up at the singing rooster on the tree.

The fox blinked his eyes over and over again with disbelief. He had been confident that he was going to be able to find something delicious for breakfast, but this was a real dream come true. Saliva began to drool from the corners of his snout.

At first, the rooster hadn't noticed the fox looking up at him, but when he stopped singing, he heard a clapping sound coming from below him and when he looked down, he saw the fox.

The fox looked up to the rooster and said, "Wow, Mr. Rooster never in my entire life have I heard something so beautiful, so magnificent, your voice is truly a breath of fresh air. With that kind of voice you must be really famous. I feel so privileged to have heard such wonderful vocals."

The rooster's chest swelled with pride.

Then, the fox shifted his voice a little bit and said, "It's a shame that I couldn't hear you all that well because I am deaf in one ear." He feigned a look of disappointment, "Hey, Mr. Rooster do you think that you could come closer and sing to me down here so that I may hear you better?"

The rooster's head was still swimming from all of the nice compliments that he had received, but he looked down to the fox and replied, "Sure no problem, but first you have to ask my friend if it's ok, he is asleep there in that hole on the button of the tree, and if he says that it's ok, then I will gladly come down and sing for you."

The fox went over to the hole and slowly peeked in and at that precise moment, a giant dog came out barking at the fox, almost tearing his head off. The fox, scared nearly half to death turned around and ran as fast as he possibly could in the opposite direction and disappeared into the thick undergrowth.

Lesson: If you want to survive in the business world or the corporate world, or anywhere really, you have to be like the rooster and use your smarts and awareness skills. Remember: there are lots of foxes out there, just waiting to take advantage of you

The Fisherman

Every morning, on his way to work, a local businessman would notice a fisherman by the lake. The fisherman would be there every day with his fishing pole trying to catch fish and, occasionally the businessman would also see the fisherman in the afternoon on his way home from work.

One afternoon he decided to stop and talk with the fisherman.

So he parked his car, got out and walked over to the pier to ask him how he was doing. After some friendly chit chat, the businessman quickly learned that fishing is how the man provided food for his family. The fisherman proceeds to tell him that sometimes it would take all day, but eventually he would catch a couple of fish to take home in order to feed his family.

The businessman was stunned that in such a modern era someone could live like this, so he gave the fisherman a great suggestion. The idea was to build a type of trap so that he wouldn't have to spend all day at the lake trying to catch just one fish. And the best part was that he could leave the trap in the mornings and come back for the fish in the evenings.

But the fisherman didn't know how to make such traps. However, being an eclectic designer, the business man did, so he drew a rough blueprint on the sand for the fisherman. The trap was simple enough; all that he was going to need was a little bit of wood, a couple of nails and a small net.

So the next day the fisherman got everything that he needed and he set out to make his trap. When the trap was ready he positioned the trap in the water and went back home to take a nap.

Late afternoon, when he got up from his nap, he went to check on his trap and was pleasantly surprised to see that he had caught some fish. As a matter of fact, he caught ten times more fish then he would have by only using a fishing pole. He was so glad that the businessman had given him this idea because now, he could feed his family even more fish than before and the best part was that he wasn't going to have to spend all day trying to catch fish. Even though fishing was his favorite hobby in the whole world, but now he was going to have time for other things...more important things; like spending time with his family.

But there was one problem, they couldn't eat all of the fish that he had caught in the trap and since they were very humble, the family didn't have a refrigerator and so, unavoidably, the uneaten fish went to waste.

The fisherman decided that the best thing to do was to go down to the local electronics store and buy his family a refrigerator so that they could store the fish. He was sad to find out that the small amount of money he had saved was not enough to buy a refrigerator and so the fisherman, with the little money he had, decided to buy some work clothes and get a job, so that he could make enough money to buy a refrigerator.

After several long months of hard work and penny pinching finally he saved enough money to buy his refrigerator. The fisherman was very happy because now, not only could he catch fish in bulk, but he could also preserve them. Now his family wouldn't have to worry about food for days.

The fisherman didn't have to work anymore because now he already had what he wanted, his refrigerator. But after a couple of months of having the refrigerator he got an extremely expensive electric bill. He almost feinted when he saw it. Regrettably, the fisherman had to go back to work in order to save up enough money to pay the electric bill.

Soon after that, the fisherman had time for nothing else; he had to work all the time in order to pay the bills, so he no longer had any time for fishing or even setting the traps, so it became easier for him to just buy fish at the local market.

The fisherman lived a very unhappy life after that; he never had any time for his family because he was always working in order to buy fish and pay bills.

Lesson: Remember that everything comes at the price of something else. No real benefit ever comes without a true sacrifice.

A Boy and a Rock Stand

One morning a young lad set up a stand at the end of his driveway. He collected rocks from his yard and put them on display around his stand; the goal was simple…he was going to sell the rocks.

In the afternoon, the boy's father comes home from work and after parking the car in the garage he walks over to his son and asks him what he was doing. The little boy explains to his father that he was selling rocks. Feeling a little confused the father looked down at the boy and then at the stand.

He tried to explain to his son that no one was going to buy rocks. That it was a better idea to set up a lemonade stand or something, anything but rocks because no one was going to buy his rocks.

The little boy didn't want to sell lemonade; he wanted to sell rocks, so he told his father that he had a better chance of selling the rocks. The father shrugged his head and walked away thinking of how stubborn his son was, "Got that from his mother." He thought, as he walked into the house.

So every morning the little boy set up his stand to sell his rocks and day after day no one came to buy any rocks. Obviously the father thought all of this to be ridiculous; so one day, when he came home from work, he thought he would try once more to talk his son out of this madness.

He explained to him yet again that no one was going to buy dirty old rocks and that it would be easier to sell something that everyone liked or needed. He offered his son several good ideas of things that he could sell.

But the boy was committed to selling his

rocks.

The father kneeled down to look into his son's eyes and said, "Son, please believe me when I tell you that you are not going to be able to sell any of these rocks."

The little boy looked back into his father's eyes and said, "Dad, please believe me when I tell you that I am going to sell everyone of these rocks."

The father saw that there was no way he was going to convince his son, so he gave up and went back into the house. He decided that he would let his son, learn for himself, the reality of the unforgiving business world. He thought that sooner or later his son would have to learn how to deal with failure anyway.

So every day the little boy set up his stand and everyday hardly anyone drove by and the ones that did showed absolutely no interest in buying any of his rocks. But the little boy didn't give up and everyday he came back even more determined to sell his rocks.

Then one day, a car came up the street towards the little boy's stand. At first the little boy thought that they might be lost looking for directions but then, a woman came out of the passenger's door and walked over to the little boy. She was looking for some rocks to put around her garden and asked him how much he wanted for the rocks. He told the lady the rocks were a dollar a piece and the woman took out her purse and bought every single rock he had.

Then, the little boy went back into the house and when his father asked him why he was no longer at his rock stand the little boy explained that he had already sold all the rocks and took out a wad of bills to show his father.

Entirely proud of himself, he looked at his father and said, "I told you that I was going to sell all of my rocks. I knew that it was going to happen sooner or later because I strongly believe that I can do anything that I put my mind to do." With that the little boy turned to go to his room in order to get ready for lunch.

The father was left speechless on the couch.

Lesson: If you believe in something strong enough and hard enough, then you will be able to achieve it. Like the old saying goes: what the heart believes and the mind perceives, then you can achieve.

Bear and Fish

A photographer for the national geographic was assigned to take pictures of the black bears of the Colorado Mountains. The photographer had already taken hundreds of pictures of the bears in their natural environment and on the final day of shooting, decided that he would take some last pictures of the bears down by the river.

When he got to the river he was surprised to find that there was a bear standing waste deep in the middle of the river. The bear appeared to be catching fish.

The photographer observed something very unique and fortunately, was able to capture it on film.

The bear had already caught several small fish and had all of them tucked under one giant arm. All of sudden, the bear caught sight of a huge fish swimming around his massive legs. The bear seemed undecided as to what to do next; it was obvious that he wanted to catch the giant fish but he was going to need both hands in order to accomplish that feat. So the bear switched his glance multiple times, from the tiny fish under his arm to the big fish that he wanted to catch.

It was as though the bear, in that moment, was weighing the options of dropping the smaller fish to try to go for the big one. Then the big fish, as though it could somehow feel that its life was in danger, swam quickly away to safety.

The bear looked at the fish's massive shadow under the water, as it swam further and further away.

Lesson: If you want to achieve greatness in your life, you first have to be willing to get rid of the small things that you keep holding onto.

The Car

One of the largest direct sales companies in the world held a conference call in the beginning of the New Year with all of their sales managers on the national level. The owner of the company announced that there was going to be a competition in which the winner was going to win a brand new, forty thousand dollar luxury BMW. To qualify to win the car you had to have the biggest and most productive sales team in the country and in September, during a national convention, the car would be awarded to the winner.

From the moment he hang up the phone Brian knew that he was going to win the car.

Not because he had the biggest and most productive sales team in the company, as a matter of fact, he was currently the only member on his sales team. Needless to say, he had a lot of growing to do; so winning the car, at that point, was a long shot at best. But nevertheless, he was confident that he was going to win that car.

He wrote a small note to himself and stuck it in his wallet, it read: I will win the car. Then he opened his agenda and on every single date leading up to the end of September he wrote in the words, I will win the car.

He changed his desktop wallpaper on his computer to read: I will win the car.

In his bathroom mirror at home, he put a little note to remind himself that he was going to win the car. He put post ums all over the house that reminded him that he was going to win the car; he also put them on his TV, on the fridge, the toilet, the sink, the cabinets, on his bowling ball, his golf clubs, and even his high school year book, that he hadn't opened in more than five years.

Everywhere you looked in his home there

were small signs that reminded you that Brian was going to win the car. As if that weren't enough, all he could talk about with his friends and family members was how he was going to win that car.

All day long, to his colleagues at work, that was all he talked about as well.

In order to reach his goal he worked around the clock without ever getting tired and even at the slightest yawn, he would just look at his giant BMW poster, that he put up in his cubicle, he would quickly be motivated to back to work.

Then September finally rolled around and everyone was ready for the convention.

Brian brought as many people as he possibly could, friends, family, girlfriend, co-workers everyone and anyone who wanted to come he brought, because he wanted everyone to see him winning that car.

Finally, at the end of the convention they unveiled the BMW and every person in the auditorium oohooed and wowwed. Everyone held their collective breaths as they were about to announce the winner.

With the exception to Brian, everyone was surprised when his name was called out.

Lesson: When you fall in love and truly believe in an idea watch out! There is nothing that you won't be able to do, because the mind is a very powerful thing and whatever your mind truly desires you will get.

Eye of the Tiger

Tom loves to wrestle. As a matter of fact, there isn't a single thing that he doesn't enjoy about the sport; he loves the sweat, the blood, the bruises and most of all, he loves to win. Tom is a winner.

One winter, Tom entered a state wide wrestling competition and made it easily through the preliminaries to advance on to the tougher stages. In this competition, Tom was the wrestler to beat. He was favored to win his weight class of one hundred and sixty five pounds.

Tom was beating opponents one after another and before long he was in the semifinal match where the winner would advance to the finals; once there, he would have the opportunity to compete for the title of best wrestler, in that weight class, in the entire state.

The semi-final match was a little tougher then Tom had expected but nevertheless, he made it through and was thrilled to find himself moving on to the finals. Tom invited everyone to come to see him; friends, family members and he even invited his girlfriend who had never been to one of his matches because she found wrestling to be too barbaric and distasteful. This was a huge event for everyone involved, but especially for Tom. This was going to be his first finals ever and needless to say, he was a bit nervous. With his adrenaline on high alert, on the night before the match he barely got any sleep, he was just too excited.

By the time the match was getting ready to start, Tom had thrown up more than three times. He was extremely nervous.

When the time came for his turn to wrestle, Tom felt as though he were going to feint. But he was still pretty confident; after all, he had beaten many tough wrestlers in order to make it to the final, so he knew that he deserved to be there and so he was optimistic about pulling out a win, but it all changed when he saw his opponent.

Tom couldn't believe that his opponent was in the same weight class as him because the guy was enormous. Built like a house, the guy was made of pure muscle. To make matters worse, he looked really scary, had a real mean gaze and everything. The guy looked like a cross between a human and a giant pit-bull.

The referee summoned both wrestlers to the middle of the mat and briefly went over the rules of the match and then the two wrestlers shook hands, the referee blew his whistle and the match was on. In the blink of an eye, the human pit-bull was all over Tom like white on rice and in just a matter of seconds, had him pinned down to the mat. The match was called in just sixteen seconds. It was a new tournament championship finals record and everyone in the stadium was shocked, Tom lost the match in record time.

When interviewed and asked about what happened, Tom simply said, "That guy didn't have to beat me, because I had already beaten myself."

Lesson: Life is hard enough that you don't beat yourself into submission. This lesson we have already learned, that the mind can be your greatest ally or your worst enemy, so don't lose the fight before even stepping onto the battlefield.

The Rhino

One of the largest marketing firms in the world has a rhino as its company logo. The rhino isn't just the company's logo, but also its mascot. Everywhere you go in the company you run into the rhino in some form or another. From statues, to paintings, to t-shirts, to tattoos; everyone in the company is completely obsessed with the rhino.

When Derrick graduated from college he was hired to work for this company and sure enough it didn't take him very long to run into the whole rhino philosophy. He noticed it right away, as a matter of fact, on the very first day of work. The secretary had a rhino painted on her coffee mug; his boss had a marble statue of a rhino on his desk and that was only the beginning.

The young man had his curiosity peeked, so he asked the head of his department the reason why everyone was so fascinated with the rhino.

The department boss shook his head and began to tell the rookie employee the significance behind the rhino.

He explained to him in detail why the rhino was so important to the company; that it was because of their three inch thick skin, their horn, the fact that they were incapable of going backwards and the fact that rhino's don't have good peripheral vision, they could only see straight forward and not sideways.

The rookie employee asked him how this related to the world of advertising and sales. The department head explained it to him.

"Well, if you have a three inch thick skin, then no negative can penetrate you, if you had a horn, then you would be able to break through any obstacle and like the rhino, we must never go backwards only forwards and finally, we must only be able see what's in front and never sideways so that way, we never get sidetracked from our goals."

From that day on that rookie employee became the rhino's most faithful follower.

Lesson: Always keep your mind focused on your objectives. Never get distracted because it's easier to go down the road of failure, then to get across the path to success.

Lottery Ticket

Larry was a privileged man and he always felt like he was the luckiest person in the world. His entire life he had been gifted with one fortunate situation after another. He was extremely blessed when it came to love, always having the most beautiful girlfriends amongst his friends. He was also lucky in school, because for some reason or another, the teachers always favored him. In addition, Larry had never worked a day in his adult life, but somehow money always seemed to find its way into his pockets, so he was never broke. Also, Larry was gifted with the best group of friends that anyone could wish for.

One day, while Larry was still in school, he decided to try his luck in something that was very hard to win: the state lottery.

So he went to a local convenient store, placed his numbers and bought his ticket. He was extremely optimistic about winning, but his friends advised him not to get his hopes up because the odds of winning the lottery were somewhere around a billion to one. So the likelihood of luck being on his side this time was very much against him. One of his friends, Mike, had bought lottery tickets hundreds of times and hadn't won as much as five dollars, so he too told Larry not to get his hopes up.

That night, Larry watched the news to listen for the winning numbers and sure enough he won the lottery, a jackpot of ten million dollars, Larry became a millionaire over night and now, could afford to buy anything that he ever wanted.

In the beginning, his friends were happy for him, but as fate would have it, that sentiment quickly turned into envy and jealousy. Silently, amongst themselves they complained that it just wasn't fair that someone that hadn't worked a day in his life and hadn't suffered a single woe could be so fortunate. Most of them had gone through many negative situations to be where they were and still, even the best of them, only earned a little more than minimal wage and now their friend, without any effort what so ever, wins the state's biggest lottery pot in recent years; they were festering with envy and anger.

They came to the general consensus that their friend was by far the luckiest person on the face of the planet.

When Larry first got his money, he did what anyone with so much money would do; he dropped out of school and bought himself a huge mansion in a posh, affluent neighborhood. It wasn't long before Larry was living the life of the rich and famous; buying expensive cars and Rolex watches, the whole nine yards. As it were, he had a maid or servant for everything, all in all, employing over a dozen people to do even the most mundane tasks.

Before long, Larry was spending hundreds of thousands of dollars of month; then, he started getting into the habit of hiring prostitutes and things really went downhill from there. One of his usual girls was heavily into drugs and it wasn't long before Larry also began doing drugs and within a couple of years he had himself a, ten thousand dollars a week, drug habit.

Larry thought that his money would last forever but that wasn't the case and it wasn't long before he began to have financial problems. Well, at first it wasn't a problem because he could simply sell one of his luxurious cars or some expensive jewelry and use that money to maintain his costly life style.

Soon enough, Larry ran out of small things to sell, so he put his multimillion dollar mansion up for sale and moved into a cheap apartment on the bad side of town. But nothing could seem to satisfy his insatiable appetite for drugs; eventually, he went through all the money that he had gotten from the sale of his mansion. Ultimately, he had to sell everything he owned, including his clothes, in order to keep up with his drug addiction.

Ten years after winning the ten million dollar lottery ticket, Larry now found himself without an education, broke, unemployed, homeless, friendless and with a nasty drug addiction. It wasn't long after that that Larry died of a drug overdose.

At his funeral someone was heard saying, "Larry was the unluckiest person that I have ever met."

Lesson: Everything in life comes with a price because nothing is free. So working hard to get what you really want is inevitable, because there are no shortcuts. Life is filled with good and bad things; unfortunately, we are always handed an equal dosage of both.

Man in the Forest

A humble farmer's son had an inquisitive mind and always asked his father all sorts of questions. One day, he goes to his father and asks him what it was that he needed to do to be successful in life.

The farmer looked at his son and shrugged his shoulder. He explained to him that they were simple country folk and didn't know such things.

The boy inquired as to who would know.

The farmer thought about it long and hard and then told him that he could probably get the answer from the town's holy man. He assured his son that the holy man was knowledgeable on all matters.

The next day, the son went into town to search out the holy man in order to find out from him how to achieve success in life.

He was informed that the holy man lived in a humble little house in the outskirts of town. The farmer's son walked over the holy man's house and knocked on the door and waited.

An old man came out holding a wooden cane.

The farmer's son introduced himself and then explained why he had come.

Unfortunately, the holy man also did not have the answer to his question because, as it turns out, he was only an expert on matters of the spirit. For example, he knew the secrets to spiritual enlightenment; but nothing of earthly wealth and economical accomplishments.

He did, however, give the young man advice as to where he could locate someone that would be able to help him find an answer to his question.

There was a rich and powerful man that

lived deep in the woods; and so the holy man instructed the farmer's son to search out the rich guy because he would know for sure how to help him.

The following day, the farmer's son set out on his journey. After a long day's walk, he finally got to the place described by the holy man.

He was standing in front of a huge gate that was made of thick wood and adorned with luxurious gold trimmings. The farmer's son looked up in amazement at the gate because it must have been at least twenty feet high if not more. There was a huge metal knob in the middle of the door.

Griped with trepidation, the young man reached for the knob. Then, as hard as he possibly could, he swung the heavy knob against the door several times. The loud thumping sound echoed aimlessly in the breadth of greenery that surrounded him.

A couple of long minutes later a man came to the door; he opened it slightly and peered through the crack. The farmer's son quickly introduced himself and explained to the man, why he was there.

When he finished, there was a short period of uncomfortable silence, but, ultimately, the man behind the door opened the door wider and halfheartedly invited the young man to come inside.

The farmer's son stepped through the door and the man asked him to follow. The young man said nothing and quietly followed the man as he walked towards the side of the house. Then the man turned and began walking towards a lake that was a couple of hundred yards away. When they got to the lake, the man walked onto a peer that extended out roughly ten feet into the lake.

When they got to the end of the peer, the man crouched down, picked up a huge cinder block and handed the cinder block to the young man.

Not understanding its intended purpose, the young man took the cinder block without question. He began to explain to the rich man that he had just come to ask him the secret of being successful and that he didn't understand what was going on.

The tycoon looked up at the young man and told him that he was going to tell him the secret to success. But first, he wanted to know if the young man was worthy of such knowledge, so he was going to put him through a test.

The young man was still confused but said nothing else.

The man told the farmer's son to jump into the water while holding the brick, explaining that he wanted to see how long he could swim while holding onto the brick.

The young man was a little hesitant but did as he was told. So he jumped feet first into the murky water and after a couple of seconds, came back up to the surface while still holding onto the heavy cinderblock. He was only able to swim, while holding the brick, for a couple of minutes, but then had to let go.

The man handed him another brick and the young man struggled to hold on, but quickly had to let go of it as well.

Then the man handed the young man a third and final brick. But the young man was simply too tired, so this time, he was only able to hold on to the brick for a mere second and immediately let go.

The old man helped the young man out of the water then turned to face him.

"The secret of being successful is that you can't hold on to the things that keep dragging you. If you want to fill your life with nothing but positives, then you have to be willing to get rid of all of the negative things in your life that keep you bogged down."

Lesson: The more you surround yourself with negativity, the more of a negative person you become, so if you want to be successful, you have to surround yourself with positive things and influences.

In the Army

A certain young man had spent the better part of his adult life wanting to be in the army. That was all he ever thought about. So for an entire year, before he was to take the ASVAB, which is the written exam given by the army, he trained. Consequently, every day he ran at least five miles in order to put himself in tip top shape for the army. In addition, he lifted weights, exercised, ate only healthy foods and he even went as far as to shave his head.

Then the day finally came for the exam. The written part of the exam the young man passed with flying colors. He needed to score a certain amount of points if he was going to qualify to be an MP; his first goal was to spend a couple of years as military police, but upon leaving the army, he would become a cop. His ultimate goal was to someday become an FBI or CIA agent.

From an elite group of one hundred and fifty other men, the young man scored third best on his exam and based on that result alone, he could qualify for any position within the army and needless to say, he was very excited about the endless possibilities the army had to offer.

The morning after the written exam, the young man had to go through a physical and this is where he ran into a problem. Everything was going according to plan that is, until he got to the hearing test. He was put into a soundproof booth and earphones were set over his ears. The test was simple enough; every time he heard a noise he was to lift his hand. The noise would vary from ear to ear and it came in form of soft beeps.

The problem was that the young man was completely deaf in his left ear, so every time the beep sounded on his left side he was not able hear it, ultimately leading him to failing this part of the physical.

At the end of the exam he was led into the office of the commander in charge and after several long awaited minutes the commander came in and explained to the young man that he was not going to be allowed into the army because of the fact that he was obviously hearing impaired.

The young man was crushed; this was a devastating blow for him. Never in his entire life had he looked upon his hearing as a handicap. He had always been able to do whatever he had put his mind to do, but now, that wasn't going to be possible and for the first time in his life, he felt like a handicap.

The young man was depressed for weeks. He just couldn't pull himself together. But then, out of nowhere, something miraculous happened. He suddenly got a full scholarship to attend college. He was selected for the scholarship from a distinct group of hundreds of applicants. His guidance counselor had sent in the application without his knowledge.

The young man ended up going to college,

getting a masters degree in marketing and went on to become one of the most important executives in one of the most powerful advertising agencies in the world. He became a millionaire, and had all of his wishes in life come true.

And it was all thanks to the fact that he was deaf in one ear.

Lesson: Sometimes it is hard to see past the negative that is in front of us; but be patient, because you never know how the story will ultimately end and sometimes in life, the biggest negative can also turn out to be your biggest positive.

The Light Bulb

Ivan ran a very successful business in Dallas. Consequently, he was training an assistant with a very promising future, named Frank. Frank seemed to possess all the necessary skills to be a great manager; the image, the smarts and most important of all, the leadership abilities.

As it were, Ivan was planning to expand his business into Houston and was looking at Frank as the best candidate to run the expansion office.

However, Frank had one major flaw; he was not very proactive and had a hard time with taking initiative when it came to doing things on his own. He lacked a lot of that. Ultimately, Frank always stood around and waited to be told what to do next. Every day he waited for Ivan to run the staff meetings and never volunteered to run them, he never asked what needed to be done next, but would rather stand around and wait to be told what to do.

Obviously, Ivan saw this significant problem as a potential for disaster because he knew that being proactive was a vital part to the success of any organization.

He tried various techniques with the hopes that Frank would catch on. But nothing did and Frank waited passively for things to happen instead of taking the bull by the horns and making them happen.

Finally one day, Ivan decides to put Frank through a final test to see if he had improved. So he went into the bathroom in the conference room and unscrewed the light bulb. This particular bathroom had no window so without a light bulb, it was utterly impossible to see even your own hand in there.

Ivan sat back and waited to see how long it

would take his assistant Frank to replace the light bulb. He waited and waited, as a matter of fact, he waited for five weeks, but Frank didn't put a new bulb in the bathroom. Ivan was unable to understand why, because everyone complained to Frank about the bathroom being too dark, but he never did anything about it.

Fed up with his apathy, Ivan calls Frank into his office and asked him why he hadn't replaced the light bulb in the bathroom; but even he didn't seem to know why he hadn't; but he just never gave it that much importance.

Needless to say, the day after that, Frank was standing out in the unemployment lines.

Lesson: Every successful company in the world is run by proactive leaders. Don't be the person that waits around for things to happen or the person that has to be told what to do all the time. Take initiative and be the guy or gal that goes out and makes things happen.

Trapped on Island

A certain day, a man took his boat out for some relaxing sailing. About three hours into his trip, out of nowhere a storm came blowing winds at more than one hundred and fifty miles per hour. Before long the ocean was throwing up waves as high as twenty feet into the air.

The man's small boat flipped upside down, subsequently, throwing him overboard into the ocean. Fortunately, he managed to find a piece of plywood to float on and, though extremely weak, was somehow able to pull himself up onto the drifting debris. He was barely conscious from the ordeal and eventually ended up passing out.

When the man came to, he found himself lying on the beach of an extremely small island.

Once he got his bearing about him, he immediately searched the island for signs of life, but quickly learned that it was completely deserted. To make matters worse, the island was literally in the middle of nowhere and so the man began to settle into the harsh reality of his situation.

In the hours that followed, the man sat on the beach thinking. He wasn't strategizing a way of staying alive; instead, he sat there thinking of all the great things in life he was going to miss out on.

He thought about how he was never going to see his friends and family again and how he was never going to eat all of his favorite foods ever again, or watch his favorite TV shows. Thinking about all of these things made him miserable and extremely sad.

But he just sat there, for hours and hours bathing in self pity and cursing God for not giving him the chance to live out a full life. There was so much more that he wanted to do and now it was evident that he was never going to get the chance to do any of those things.

Slowly but surely, as the day went on, the

man just kept thinking of more and more things that he was going to miss out on; as he did so, with each pessimistic thought, his will to live diminished. By night fall the man no longer had any desire whatsoever to live.

He couldn't or simply wasn't willing to live out a life where he wouldn't be able to do all the things that he was so passionate about. He was convinced that he didn't want to spend the rest of his life rotting on a deserted island and just like that the man completely gave up on life. Over and over again he told himself that he did not want to live and shook his fist at God for his cursed predicament.

Hours went by and thoughts of death, was all the man could think about. God must have heard his vehement diatribe in the dark because all of a sudden, the man had a massive heart attack and immediately died.

The following morning a fisherman, from a nearby island, came out to check on some of his fishing traps nearby and noticed the body of the deceased man on the beach. He looked down on the man and noticed that he had his hand clutched over his chest. The fisherman couldn't help but to wonder how many years the now diseased man had been marooned on the island.

Lesson: Staying positive is the best medicine for anything. Thinking negative thoughts is like a cancer and if you don't get rid of it right away, eventually it will grow and then it will consume you altogether.

Money on Ceiling

A CEO of a major company walked into the boardroom and told the executives to stand up. Instead of doing the usual meeting sitting down, the way it's always done, today they were going to do something a bit more unconventional and different. The CEO wanted to get his executives brainstorming different methods of making the company stronger; he came up with a dynamic presentation.

When they were all standing up, he asked them to move the chairs and table to one side and they did as they were told.

Then the CEO took out a quarter from his pocket and told everyone to look at the quarter, which they all did, not really knowing where he was headed with the demonstration.

Giving them a stern look he says, "Imagine that I take this quarter and I tape it to the ceiling." In silence they all stared into the ceiling of the boardroom, the ceiling was a good fifteen feet high if not higher.

Then the CEO called the shortest executive, in the room, to come and stand by his side.

"Now imagine we all ask Jim here to retrieve the quarter for us." He paused for one minute, giving them time to think about what he was saying. "Do you think that he could do it?"

Again the executives looked up at the ceiling as though the quarter were already there. Then they looked down to short little Jim and in unison came to the conclusion that it couldn't be done.

"He is just too short," they said in one voice.

Shooting them a blazing look, the CEO said, "What if Jim brought in a ladder, or got a piggy back ride from someone who was tall, then do you think that he could do it?"

The executives thought about it for a long second and one of them responded that it could be done, but another executive responded that the quarter just wasn't worth the hassle.

Silently, but effectively, the other executives agreed as well that the quarter just wasn't worth all the trouble.

The CEO turned to them and said, "Then what if we put ten one hundred dollar bills in an envelope and tape the envelope to the ceiling, would that be worth all the trouble?"

The executives discussed amongst themselves and came to the immediate conclusion that for one thousand dollars it would definitely be worth the trouble.

"Exactly," said the CEO. "Remember, no one will go that extra mile, if their goal is too small, so in order to get everyone working harder and smarter, we have to set higher standards and goals."

Lesson: Most people will only work as hard as they should and not as hard as they can; so set higher objectives for yourself, because when you raise the bar, you will be surprised at the things that you will be willing to do, in order to achieve your goal.

The End

Another Great Book

<u>**You Can Do It**</u>

Ivan King

"There are two ways of spreading light: to be the candle or the mirror that reflects it."

Edith Wharton

Good Things Take Time

Ivan King

Excerpt From Another Great Book

The Path

Ivan King

In order for you to fully understand my journey, we have to go back; we have to start from the very beginning, we have to return to the path……

One day, a boy was playing on the beach with his inflatable ball. His mom and dad sat nearby, sunbathing on old wooden chairs. They were just like any other family, enjoying a warm day at the beach and having some fun in the sun.

"Mom," the boy yelled out. "Look at what I can do!" The mom paid him no mind. "That's nice dear," she would say without so much as looking at the poor lad. His cries for attention fell on deaf ears. "Mom!" Shouted the precocious boy, "But you're not even looking!" Then he crossed his arms and pouted his lips.

"That's silly," she replied while still not taking the time to see what he was up to. "I see you," she continued, "You're such a big boy now, look at what you can do with that ball!" Then, for the first time all afternoon, she took a peak to see what in the world her son was doing. "You're my special little guy," she said to him with a half grin.

"Mom," he screamed at her. "You keep saying that, but it's not true. I'm not little anymore; I'm big now!" Then, with the metaphorical force of a six hundred pound gorilla he kicked the ball far, far away.

"Well, no matter how big you get, you will always be my little guy." Then she pointed a hard finger at him and said, "Now, you go get that ball mister and when you return I want you to start behaving yourself." He shot her an angry stare; as mean of a look as he could muster. "Do I need to repeat myself?" She looked at him as her tone rose to an all familiar pitch. "Or, would you rather I wake up your father?"

"No," he said promptly. "Don't wake dad, I'll go get the ball." He was old enough to understand he had been defeated.

"When you return," she continued with his scolding. "We're going to have a nice little chat about your attitude." He didn't dare say anything back at her. "Did you hear me?" She asked with a stern look.

"Yes," he responded sounding dejected. "I'll go get the ball."

"And then what?" She asked with a smoldering look that sent a chill running down his spine.

"And then I'll start behaving," he said unwittingly, and kicked up the sand around his feet in a last fit of defiance.

"You see," she said with a soft smile. "Now, that wasn't so hard." She lowered her sunglasses slightly in order to get a better look at him and said, "Make sure you stay close, I don't want you wandering off." He gave her an insolent look but kept silent; he knew better than to challenge her when she was in the wrong sort of mood. "Did you hear what I said?" she asked.

"Yes!" He blurted out and stomped his feet, "I heard you a thousand times already." He hated when she got like this. She didn't say anything to him, she didn't have to. All she had to do was stare at him with that look, it was the mom look. He shrugged his shoulders and winced; his hard stare faded away like ice cream in the melting sun. "Yes Ma'am," he said tamely and quickly retreated to fetch his ball.

At the edge of the beach, where the warmth of the soft sand met with the cold hard earth, there were small dusty dunes littered with dried grass that stood about knee high. The boy noticed that between two of these dunes, there was a narrow sandy path about the width of his shoulders. This path led to the abandoned field where the ball had been kicked. He made his way to the mouth of the path in a hurry; once there, he bobbed his head around looking for it, and quickly spotted it. The colorful ball stood out like a sore thumb in the desiccated landscape; the red, blue and green stripes were an eyesore against the backdrop of the sundried meadow.

Download Today on Amazon.com

The Path

Ivan King

Ivan King Library

The Path

Breakfast With Jesus

Hell: A Place Without Hope

The Dark Room

The Blue Gumball

Good Things Take Time

You Can Do It

Meet the Author

Ivan King was born in Rio de Janeiro, Brazil, in 1977, though his stay in Rio was to be short lived. Adopted from an orphanage, he was raised in Ipatinga's, Valley of Steel. His favorite author is Hemingway; yet his favorite book, is Steinbeck's Grapes of Wrath. When he is not writing or reading, he plays chess and the guitar.

When Ivan was eight, he read his first book, Judy Blume's Superfudge and the rest is history. That's the story behind how the passion for reading began; how it ends...has yet to be written.

Currently, he is working on a couple dozen writing projects and turning some of his novels into screenplays. Ivan's first published work, The Dark Room, is a Fiction Novel loosely based on his life growing up in the favelas, or slums, of Brazil.

Favorite quote: "In life, incredible things happen and unforgettable moments do exist; but nothing compares to having been loved by you, and though you rest in peace, I will miss and love you always."

If you would like to learn more about Ivan King, you can send him a message at:

http://www.ivanking.com/

Made in United States
Orlando, FL
19 August 2022